CONDUCTING LAWFUL TERMINATIONS

FRANCIS T. COLEMAN

Coleman, Coxson, Penello,
Fogleman & Cowen
A Professional Corporation

1000 Vermont Avenue, N.W.
Suite 600
Washington, D.C. 20005

SHRM FOUNDATION
SOCIETY FOR HUMAN RESOURCE MANAGEMENT

ISBN 0-939900-67-X

This book is published by the Society for Human Resource Management and was funded by a grant from the SHRM Foundation. The interpretations, conclusions, and recommendations, however, are those of the author, and do not necessarily represent those of the Foundation or of SHRM.

Francis T. Coleman
Coleman, Coxson, Penello, Fogleman & Cowen, P.C.

Francis (Tom) Coleman, born in Washington, DC, founding principal, Coleman, Coxson, Penello, Fogleman & Cowen, P.C., Judge Advocate Program, U.S. Marine Corps 1964-1967, Adjunct Professor, Georgetown Law Center 1971-1980, member of labor and employment law sections of the American Bar Association, Federal Bar Association, District of Columbia Bar Association and Maryland Bar Association. Past Chairman of the American Society for Association Executives' Legal Section; past Chairman of the CUE Labor Lawyers Advisory Committee (a subsidiary of National Association of Manufacturers (NAM)). A member of the Board of Directors and current Chairman of the Small and Solo Practice Committee of the Bar Association of the District of Columbia; listed in Who's Who Professional Registry and included in the first edition of "The Best Lawyers in America."

Mr. Coleman received A.B., L.L.B. and Masters of Labor Law degrees from Georgetown University, where he was the recipient of the first John F. Kennedy Labor Law Award.

CONTENTS

CHAPTER I

THE EMPLOYMENT TERMINATION DECISION

Discharge or termination of employment, the key employee rights issue of the 1990s, is justifiably referred to as "the capital punishment of the workplace." The disruptive impact that the termination decision can have on employees and employers alike has been well-chronicled.

In his *Termination Handbook*, Robert Coulson observed:

> Many managers and workers who are involved in employment terminations are floundering, ignorant of the legal rights of employers and employees, unaware that the rules are changing, insensitive to the trauma of losing a job. I have seen too many cases where people's careers have been blighted because of such miscalculations. Someone was discharged without cause; the executive who did the firing was held accountable. An employee who should have been terminated was kept on the job; morale in the office plummeted. A dispute over a termination found its way into court; both parties suffered. (*The Termination Handbook*, MacMillan Publishing Co. (1981), pp. vii-viii.)

Written in 1981, these observations are just as valid today. Many managers are still floundering in their attempts to terminate undesirable and unproductive employees and to make those discharges "stick." Too many managers have found out the hard way that terminating employees for productivity, competency or disciplinary reasons can have significant consequences for those involved in the decision making process as well as for the affected employees. Recent headlines taken from newspapers nationwide show the tremendous costs at stake in making those types of termination and layoff decisions:

- Former Westinghouse Workers Win Age Discrimination Ruling in Dispute Over Maryland Layoffs

- Ex-Workers Hit Back with Age-Bias Suits
- Big Changes Likely as Law Bans Bias Toward Disabled
- Blacks Are Seeking $58 Million for Alleged Pattern of Discrimination
- Parent Firm Can Be Sued for Subsidiary's Layoffs
- Former Employee Receives $650,000 Damages After Discharge for "Whistle Blowing"
- Leading San Francisco Department Store Ordered to Pay Over $1.3 Million in Age Discrimination Case
- Company Ordered to Pay Millions, Individual Supervisors Thousands, in Sexual Harassment Suit
- General Motors Settles Discrimination Case for $42.5 Million
- Bank Agrees to Pay $14 Million in Back Wages to Settle Discrimination Suit Filed on Behalf of Women and Minorities

Those headlines are being repeated throughout the country almost every day. Small- to medium-sized employers are suffering the same devastating financial consequences as their *Fortune* 500 counterparts in termination lawsuits filed by former employees. Research studies show that the average damage award in a wrongful discharge case in 1988 was $311,332 and the private employee bringing a wrongful discharge claim had an 86 percent chance of winning. (The July 1989 issue of *Nations Business* provides an excellent discussion of the high cost of litigating wrongful discharge and other employment cases.) Any decision to involuntarily terminate an employee has the potential to inflict disastrous consequences on a company's financial well-being. Accordingly, managers at all levels should be asking themselves: "What steps can we take to protect ourselves from the potentially devastating legal consequences of a layoff or termination while still eliminating undesirable and unproductive employees?"

Consequences for Employers

Although all employment decisions have potential legal consequences, the decision to discharge an employee creates the greatest potential financial liability for the employer. In most instances, the potential backpay meter starts to tick from the moment of termination, and because resolution of any claim is likely to be years away, an employer may find itself facing a substantial backpay award many years after the discharge itself took place.

Court orders also frequently include compensatory or punitive damages as well as backpay. The 1991 amendments to the Civil Rights Act of 1964 provide for such damages ranging in amounts from $50,000 to $300,000, depending on the size of the employer's workforce. Furthermore, if the ex-employee's claim is upheld, judicial and administrative relief will generally include not only full backpay, but also reinstatement to the employee's former job. The terminated employee's return to his or her former position could have quite a disruptive impact on the workforce.

Obviously, avoiding these highly undesirable consequences should be a top priority of any HR manager. Yet, hesitancy or failure to separate an undesirable or unproductive employee from the employer's payroll may prove almost as costly as an ill-advised termination. This is the dilemma confronting today's managers.

Changing Nature of the Employment-At-Will Relationship

The employment-at-will doctrine provides that an employee hired for an unspecified period of time may be terminated at any time and for any reason. Under this traditional legal concept, it is often said that an employee can be fired for any reason—whether a good reason, a bad reason, or no reason at all. In recent years, however, the employment-at-will doctrine has been eroded by federal and state legislatures and by the courts to the point where it is practically unrecognizable.

Federal Legislative Limitations

The first major legislative inroad limiting the employment-at-will doctrine occurred during the mid-1930s when Congress passed the National Labor Relations Act, which prohibited employers from discriminating against employees on the basis of concerted protected activity. This law is generally regarded as protecting union activity but, in fact, it is much broader. It also protects group conduct or activity directed to wages, hours or working conditions.

In the mid-1960s, Congress passed Title VII of the Civil Rights Act of 1964 (42 U.S.C. § 2000(e)), which further limited the employment-at-will doctrine by prohibiting discrimination in employment on the basis of race, creed, color, national origin or sex. In 1967, Congress added age discrimination to the list of illegal employer decision-making factors by passing the Age Discrimination in Employment Act (29 U.S.C. § 621 (1967)). This law added a new protected category, employees 40 and older. In 1973, Congress enacted the Vocational Rehabilitation Act (29 U.S.C. § 706 (1973)), which prohibits discrimination on the basis of handicap by employers receiving federal financial assistance. The Americans with Disabilities Act of 1990 (42 U.S.C. § 12101 (1990)) has added disability to the class of categories protected by Title VII, adding yet another basis for challenging an employer's termination decision.

Other statutes have subsequently been passed that protect employees from retaliatory firings for filing claims under the Employee Retirement Income Security Act (29 U.S.C. § 1001 (1974)), the Occupational Safety and Health Act (29 U.S.C. § 651 (1970)), the Fair Labor Standards Act (29 U.S.C. § 201 (1938)), the Family and Medical Leave Act (29 U.S.C. § 825 (1993)) or claims for Workers' Compensation. Those statutes have further limited the traditional at-will-employment doctrine and have given employees numerous additional grounds for challenging any termination decision.

State Legislative Limitations

Statutes protecting employee rights, and thereby limiting management's decision-making freedom, have been enacted at the state and local government levels as well. Such statutes frequently parallel their federal counterparts, and often expand on federal protections. Frequently, these state and local laws extend coverage to employers who might not be covered under their federal law counterparts.

Judicial Limitations

In addition to an increasing number of legislative constraints on management's freedom to fire, judicial decisions have steadily eroded the right of employers to discharge at-will employees by adopting limitations on an employer's right to terminate employees. With increasing regularity, courts are overturning employee terminations on a variety of legal theories. (See Chapter III.)

Coping with the Shrinking Employment-At-Will Doctrine

Increasingly, employers are perplexed by the maze of laws restricting their right to make important employment decisions such as termination. Often, fear of the unknown consequences of a termination have paralyzed employers' decision making ability. Despite these legal developments, however, employers can still retain the right to control their workforces by following the simple principles set forth in Chapter IV. Through the use of sound judgment, and by investigating before rather than after a termination, management can reduce the likelihood that a termination decision is inappropriate or will later be overturned by a court or administrative agency.

Approaching the Termination Decision

Because termination decisions have enormous consequences in terms of potential monetary loss and personal anxiety, both for the employer and the employee, discharge decisions should be approached with caution and preceded by a thorough investigation and careful reflection. As the preceding discussion makes clear, these decisions cannot be taken lightly. Employees have an increasing number of legal avenues available to them for challenging their termination and they are becoming much more aware of their legal recourses. Also, there is a growing cadre of plaintiff's employment lawyers who are all too eager to educate both employees and ex-employees on how to legally challenge their employers' actions.

CHAPTER II

WHAT EMPLOYERS NEED TO KNOW ABOUT PROTECTED CATEGORY EMPLOYEES

A number of federal laws have created "protected categories" of employees. Individuals who fit into these categories and believe they have been victims of job-related discrimination can file a complaint with a federal agency, the EEOC, and can also seek relief in federal court. Title VII of the Civil Rights Act of 1964 prohibits employers from discriminating on the basis of race, creed, color, national origin or sex. The Age Discrimination in Employment Act of 1978 (ADEA) prohibits employers from discriminating against individuals age 40 and over on the basis of their age. Under the new Americans with Disabilities Act (ADA), employers with 15 or more employees not only are prohibited from discriminating against applicants and employees with a disability, but also have an affirmative duty to reasonably accommodate a disability as long as it does not result in undue hardship to the employer.

State, county and municipal laws create numerous additional protected categories of employees. The District of Columbia's Human Rights Act (D.C. Code Ann. § 1-2512 (1981)) is typical of these state and local anti-discrimination statutes, which protect a wide range of employees and prospective employees. The District of Columbia law prohibits employment discrimination for any reason other than that of individual merit, including, but not limited to discrimination "by reasons of race, color, religion, national origin, sex, age, marital status, personal appearance, sexual orientation, family responsibilities, matriculation, political affiliation, physical handicap, source of income, and place of residence or business."

Anti-Retaliation Provisions

Almost all federal, state, county and municipal anti-discrimination laws contain anti-retaliation provisions designed to protect employees who exercise or seek to exercise their rights under the laws. Employees who file charges under one or more of those laws, and are later terminated, may claim that they were discharged or laid off in retaliation for their earlier attempts to seek the protections of those laws. A retaliation claim is *separate* from the initial claim of discrimination. Indeed, an employee may have his or her initial claim of discrimination dismissed and still prevail on a charge of retaliation relating to the filing of that claim.

Individuals who fall into a protected category have easy access to federal, state and local civil rights agencies. They can use those agencies to file discrimination charges without cost to themselves. Once the charges are filed, employers will be put to the expense and inconvenience of filing a response and undergoing an investigation. Thus, before any final decision on discharge or layoff is made, employers should take into consideration whether the individual in question falls into a protected category and, if so, whether he or she has grounds to support a claim of discrimination.

Assessing Discrimination Claims

Both the administrative agencies and the courts use two basic legal theories to assess the merits of a discrimination claim: disparate treatment and disparate impact. Employers should be aware that regardless of the specific allegations of any discrimination charge leveled against them, the ensuing Title VII investigation will be based on one or both of those legal theories.

Disparate treatment occurs when employers treat an employee who is a member of a protected category differently than they treat non-protected category employees with respect to the same type of employment decision. For instance, the fact that an employer imposes more severe discipline on a black employee than a white employee charged with the same infraction may result in a claim of disparate treatment discrimination. If a protected category employee can demonstrate that he or she was treated more harshly than a non-protected category employee under the same or similar circumstances, the employer will be called upon to justify the dissimilar treatment.

To ensure they will be prepared to defend against a disparate treatment discrimination claim, employers must accurately document the job performance of all employees. By keeping accurate, complete records, employers will be in a position to properly distinguish one employee's work record from another's if a disparate treatment claim is filed. In the case of a discharge, for example, if an employer can show that non-protected category employees have been terminated for the same or similar offenses as the protected category employee, the employer is much more likely to prevail. Consistency in treatment is critical in defending against "disparate treatment" discrimination claims.

Disparate impact involves the application of rules or standards that, while not discriminatory on their face, may have a disparate impact on protected category employees. Classic examples are height and weight restrictions, which often exclude from job opportunities a greater proportion of females than males. Similarly, imposing certain educational requirements on job applicants may have a disparate impact on minority applicants by disqualifying a disproportionate number of them. If a job requirement has a disparate impact on protected category employees, and if it is not reasonably related to the job in question, then the requirement may be found to be unlawful discrimination. To protect against such potential liability, employers must make sure that any job requirements they impose are reasonably related to the performance of the job.

Civil Rights Act Remedies Broadened

In 1991, the Civil Rights Act of 1964 was amended in several ways. First, the remedies available to employees under the act were broadened to include compensatory and punitive damages. Those sources of recovery are in addition to the prospect of having to reinstate the employee, and to pay backpay and attorneys' fees. The compensatory and punitive damages available to employees range from $50,000 to $300,000, depending on the size of the employer. Those additional remedies make potential clients alleging discriminatory discharge or layoff much more attractive to plaintiff's lawyers, who will share in any monetary awards received by the employee. Indeed, the monetary incentives will often cause a plaintiff's attorney to bypass the EEOC administrative process and file suit in federal court. Thus, the 1991 amendments make it much more likely that protected category employees challenging their termination on grounds of discrimination will seek vindication through the courts rather than through the EEOC.

The 1991 amendments to Title VII, in addition to reversing several recent Supreme Court decisions having to do with procedural issues, also provide that plaintiffs in Title VII lawsuits are entitled to a trial by jury. The right to a jury trial adds an additional expense to the defense of such claims—and a greater uncertainty regarding the outcome of the case. The Supreme Court has ruled that the compensatory and punitive damages and jury trial aspects of the 1991 amendments to Title VII are not to be applied retroactively, that is, to those charges filed before November 21, 1991 (*Landgraf v. USI Film Products,* 114 S.Ct. 1483 (1994)).

Dealing with Protected Class Employees—A Word to the Wise

Employers are particularly vulnerable to attack by protected category employees through racial or sexual or ethnic remarks, jokes, slurs or other demeaning comments. If it can be shown that an employee was the victim of such comments made by managers or supervisors, or that the employer knowingly allowed protected category employees to be subjected to such oral attacks or insults from others, employers will have difficulty defending a discriminatory discharge claim. A judge, jury or administrative agency may conclude that the employer's decision to allow such conduct reflects the employer's mind-set on the subject, and that this prejudice played a role in the employee's subsequent termination. Indeed, once it is satisfactorily proven that such discriminatory communications were made or condoned, it will be almost impossible for an employer to convince a decision maker that illegal discrimination was not a factor in the termination.

A recent case involving a large financial institution in the Washington, D.C., metropolitan area illustrates the pitfalls of permitting racially, sexually or ethnically related repartee in the workplace. In this case, a former bank maintenance employee claimed his termination was racially motivated and cited remarks made by the bank's vice president of operations who he claimed referred to him as "Bubba Blackwrench" and "little black Sambo," among other racial epithets. The bank, while not denying that the remarks were made, countered that they were made in jest as part of good-natured bantering between the bank officer and the employee and that no harm was intended. The bank further claimed that the employee never objected to this "joking around" and that it was all meant in good fun. The judge hearing the case rejected the bank's defense. In fact, the judge said that the bank's decision to raise this defense underscored its insensitivity to racial prejudice and, rather than serving as a defense, constituted an aggravating factor. The damages the judge awarded against the bank emphasized his point. The lesson for employers is clear—remarks having racial, sexual or ethnic overtones, regardless of whether they are made in jest, should not be allowed in the workplace. This type of speech cannot be tolerated, unless the employer is willing to pay the price—substantial court awards for punitive damages.

The above observations apply to comments made about characteristics of any protected category, but particularly to comments made about an employee's age or senior status. Employees age 40 and over will be sure to remember such remarks as "old timer," part of the "over-the-hill gang," "no spring chicken" or other comments about their age and will cite them in support of their contention that age was a factor in their termination. Often such comments are enough to tip the scales in the employee's favor in an otherwise close case. Moreover, such remarks, when repeated under oath in a courtroom, lose all their humor—if they ever were humorous. They can have a devastating effect on a judge or jury, resulting in substantial backpay awards, as well as punitive and compensatory damages.

In sum, prudent employers should take appropriate steps to make sure that comments, remarks or other forms of communication bearing on protected category employees do not occur in the workplace and that all managers, supervisors and others in positions of authority are made aware of this precept as part of their training. And, when considering discipline or discharge of protected category employees, employers should determine, as part of their investigation, whether the protected employee has ever been verbally assaulted because of his or her protected category status. If employers eliminate this type of offensive speech from the workplace, employees will have less evidence to support a claim of discriminatory discharge.

Chapter III

Avoiding Wrongful Discharge Litigation

As mentioned earlier, the employment-at-will doctrine has been severely eroded over the past several decades. The sources of this erosion are both legislative and judicial. The protected categories of employees discussed in Chapter II make up the major legislative exceptions to the doctrine. In addition, the courts have propounded several bases on which the discharge decisions can be legally challenged, regardless of whether the discharged employee falls into a protected category. This chapter addresses some of the legal theories used by courts to overturn termination decisions, and provides guidance on how employers can best protect themselves from these judicially created exceptions to the employment-at-will doctrine.

Judicially Imposed Exceptions to the Employment-At-Will Doctrine

Implied Contract Exception

The most common judicially imposed exception to the employment-at-will doctrine is the *implied contract* exception. Under this theory, many courts have "interpreted" employee handbooks, written employment policies or directives and other forms of personnel guidelines, to impose contractual obligations on employers that can be enforced in court, just as any contract. Under this theory, employers are held responsible for the alleged written "commitments" they have made to employees regarding the nature, scope and duration of the employment relationship. Thus, when former employees consult an attorney to assess their legal rights and protections vis-à-vis a former employer, one of the first things the attorney will want to examine is the employee handbook, policy statements or directives, or any other written communication by the employer that arguably could constitute a contractual commitment. The attorney will carefully scrutinize all employer publications to determine whether employers have lived up to such "commitments," particularly when determining whether employers have followed their written procedures in terminating the employment relationship. If they have not, their actions can be challenged as a breach of the employers' implied contract with employees. Such challenges are being upheld with increasing frequency.

Employers can fight back by using the same handbooks, policy statements and directives, and other written communications to *protect* themselves from employees' claims. By including appropriate protective language in these documents, employers can shield themselves from the growing number of employment-related legal claims based on an alleged implied contract.

Employment-At-Will Disclaimers

One important form of protection against implied contract claims is the employment-at-will disclaimer. Such disclaimers should unambiguously inform both current and prospective employees that any employee can be terminated at will, in the sense that either the employer or the employee is free to terminate the employment relationship at any time and for any reason. The disclaimer also should state that no employer representative or management official has the authority to alter this at-will employment relationship, or, at least, that the at-will relationship cannot be altered except by a written document signed and dated by both the employee and a named employer representative, such as the CEO, president, or other high-ranking company official. This language may serve to protect employers from claims asserted after termination that an employer representative promised an employee some form of more permanent job security or that the employee was lured into accepting employment by promises of long-term employment or other forms of job security. Unfortunately, an employment-at-will disclaimer does not guarantee freedom from lawsuits based on an implied contract theory. Many courts look askance at these types of disclaimers and will do everything within their power to avoid giving them effect. A number of courts have rejected these disclaimers on the basis that they were not prominently displayed, that they were buried in the text of the handbook or that they were not drafted to ensure that their meaning would be clear to the employee. To overcome these objections, employers should make sure their employment-at-will disclaimers are clearly written, prominently displayed at the beginning of the manual, and highlighted or printed in bold-face type, so that it would be difficult if not impossible for anyone to contend that the information was somehow hidden from, or not understood by, the employee.

Contractual Disclaimers

Along with an employment-at-will disclaimer, employers often include a contractual disclaimer for added protection. Such a disclaimer informs employees that the personnel manual, employee handbook or other written guidelines do not constitute an employment contract, and that they are mere guidelines that can be changed at any time at the employer's discretion. Employers should be aware, however, that courts might impose restrictions on the employer's right to modify the handbook at its discretion. In an ominous decision, the South Carolina Supreme Court recently ruled that an employee handbook cannot be lawfully modified unless employees receive *actual notice* of the modification (*Fleming v. Borden, Inc.*, 450 S.E.2d 589 (1994)). To avoid claims that an employee did not have actual notice of the revision of an employee manual, employers must give all employees copies of revised manuals or policies. This is not enough, however. If a policy has been changed, the employer also should highlight the changes so that employees cannot claim that the changes were never specifically brought to their attention.

Disclaimers prominently displayed at the beginning of the employee handbook or personnel manual place current and prospective employees on notice that their continued employment is not guaranteed and can provide employers with a strong defense if their termination decisions are later challenged. The following is an example of a combined contractual and employment-at-will disclaimer:

> This handbook has been prepared to help you become familiar with your new company and to make your integration into our organization a

smooth one. It is not a contract or an agreement of employment for a definite period of time; rather, it is a summary of company policies, work rules, and the benefits you enjoy as an employee. From time to time, conditions or circumstances may require the company to change, amend, or delete some of the policies and benefits contained in this handbook. When such changes are made, the company, of course, will notify you of the new or revised policy.

All employees are employed *at will*. This means that the employees and the company are free to terminate the employment relationship at their discretion. No supervisor or other company representative has the authority to alter this relationship, and you should never interpret such person's remarks as a guarantee of continued employment. Our policy on separations is set forth more fully later in the handbook.

Such disclaimers serve the purpose of (1) specifically disavowing that the handbook is a contract; (2) informing employees that the policies contained in the handbook can be modified, altered or amended at any time; (3) spelling out the at-will nature of the employment relationship, that is, that it can be terminated by either party at any time; and (4) informing employees that no company official or representative has authority to alter or modify the at-will nature of the relationship, except as specifically set forth in the handbook.

Although a properly drafted employment-at-will and contractual disclaimer is an essential ingredient in a handbook, it is only one of many necessary protections an organization should put in place. Courts find contracts in unexpected places—not only in employees' handbooks. Creative lawyers point to such promises in employers' advertisements, recruiting brochures and application forms. The language in all these documents must be reviewed to ensure that they contain no statements that might arguably alter the employer's at-will employment relationship with its employees. A well-drafted handbook, therefore, is only the first of several steps an employer must take in protecting itself from lawsuits and other legal proceedings filed by disgruntled employees.

Acknowledgment Forms

A frequent companion to the employment-at-will and non-contractual disclaimers is an acknowledgment form that employees are asked to sign. The form reiterates the at-will nature of the employment relationship and requires the employee to acknowledge that he or she has read, understands, and will abide by the provisions of the handbook. An example of such a form follows:

> This handbook is not, nor is it intended to be, a contract of employment and is to be returned if you terminate your employment for any reason. This handbook does not restrict in any way your voluntarily leaving at any time or the right of (Name of Company) to terminate your employment at any time.
>
> If you have questions of any nature, please contact your supervisor, manager or the human resources administrator.
>
> Your signature below signifies your receipt of this handbook, your understanding of our policies, and your agreement to follow and observe them.
>
> _____(applicant's signature)
>
> _____(date)

The acknowledgment form serves to conclusively establish that the employee received the handbook and has had an opportunity to read it. The form also attests to the employee's agreement to abide by the handbook—including the statements that the handbook is not a contract and that the employee is employed at-will. It will be difficult for employees to contest those facts if they have signed an acknowledgment form.

It is not the end of the world, however, if employees refuse to sign this form. They should not be threatened or forced to sign. Rather, a notation should be made on the form that the employee was given a copy of the handbook on a certain date, but refused to sign for it. The employee's refusal to sign the receipt should be witnessed by at least two management representatives.

The acknowledgment is intended to demonstrate that the employee, in fact, received a copy of the handbook and had an opportunity to read it. Most courts agree that an organization can enforce its employment policies, even against employees who refuse to sign an acknowledgment of receipt, as long as those employees were provided with a copy of the policies.

Signed acknowledgment forms should be dated and placed in the employee's permanent personnel file. If employees refuse to sign the form, the form, with the appropriate notations, should be placed in their personnel files. This documentation could be critically important in subsequently defending the organization against lawsuits brought by present and former employees alike.

Public Policy Exceptions

Increasingly, courts are finding exceptions to the at-will employment rule based on established public policies. The theory of these cases is that, although employees otherwise might be subject to discharge at-will, they cannot be discharged for a reason that would violate an articulated public policy of the state. For instance, because sex and race discrimination in employment are both against the stated policy of the Commonwealth of Virginia, as embodied in the Virginia Human Rights Act, the Supreme Court of Virginia has ruled that the discharge of employees based on sex and race discrimination constitutes a public policy exception to the employment-at-will doctrine and that victims of such discrimination can file a claim for wrongful discharge based on state common law (*Lockhart v. Commonwealth Education Systems Corp.*, 439 S.E.2d 328 (Va. 1994)).

The significance of public policy exceptions to the at-will employment doctrine is enormous. First, of course, these exceptions interfere with the right of management to terminate an employee at will. Equally important, however, is the fact that because such claims for wrongful discharge under state common law are separate from claims based on state or federal statutory law, they are free from the limitations that restrict the statutory claims. For example, the wrongful discharge claim in *Lockhart* is not subject to the cap on compensatory and punitive damages that the 1991 amendments to the Civil Rights Act of 1964 impose in employment discrimination cases. Because wrongful discharge claims based on public policy are regarded as torts rather than contract claims, punitive damages are available to the employee. Thus, in the area of damages, the "sky's the limit" for wrongful discharge claims based on alleged violations of public policy.

Another problem with judicially crafted public policy exceptions is their unpredictability. The courts have found public policy exceptions to the at-will employment doctrine in a variety of places. In addition to anti-discrimination laws, the courts have based public policy exceptions on laws ranging from those involving workers' compensation to those involving the rights of stockholders to freely exercise their right to vote their shares. Thus, it is virtually impossible to predict where these exceptions will spring up next. Any time an employee's termination violates some arguable public policy of the state, the possibility exists that a court will uphold the employee's wrongful discharge claim—subjecting the employer to the prospects of an expensive trial and a substantial damages award.

The only way to safeguard against these claims is to consult an employment attorney before an employment termination decision. An experienced employment attorney can give employers a "quick read" on the relevant state law. They will know whether a public policy-based exception to the employment-at-will doctrine that might apply to the termination has been established in the state or is likely to be established.

Implied Covenant of Good Faith and Fair Dealing

Another basis on which courts modify the employment-at-will relationship is by imposing an *implied covenant of good faith and fair dealing* on an employer who has elected to terminate an employee. Under this theory, an employer is not free to terminate an employee at will. Rather, the employer can terminate the employee *only if* the termination is consistent with an implied obligation to deal fairly with the employee. Courts rely on this theory to amend the employment-at-will doctrine by requiring, for example, that the employer warn employees about unacceptable conduct so that they can have an opportunity to improve before they are terminated. Although generally the courts have not been receptive to this theory, employers contemplating terminating an employee should consult with an employment attorney, who can ascertain whether the courts of the relevant state have accepted this theory.

Chapter IV

Coleman's Cardinal Rules for Disciplinary Terminations

The following basic rules should be carefully followed before making a final decision to involuntarily terminate an employee for disciplinary reasons.

Rule 1: Never summarily discharge.

The first rule that every employer, regardless of size, should follow is never to summarily discharge an employee—regardless of how serious the misconduct may appear. Even when an employee is apparently caught red-handed violating a dischargeable offense rule, there is simply no reason to terminate on the spot. Appropriate discipline, including discharge, can be imposed following a disciplinary suspension that allows time for a thorough, careful investigation.

Even in circumstances where immediate discharge would appear to be in order, prudent employers will direct the employee to clock out and leave the premises. The employee will then be told that the matter will be investigated and he or she will be notified shortly as to how it will be resolved. In the meantime, the employee is "suspended subject to discharge pending further investigation." This procedure gives the employer time to take the following steps:

1. Allow time for all parties to cool down, so that an objective and dispassionate investigation may be done.
2. Take into custody and examine physical evidence, such as drugs, alcohol, stolen property.
3. Obtain written statements from all witnesses, including the employee under suspension.
4. Complete a thorough factual investigation.
5. Examine discipline previously imposed on other employees who committed similar infractions.
6. If the employee is in a protected category, determine whether he or she has been the victim of disparate

treatment or has been penalized by a rule that has a disparate impact on individuals in his or her protected category. Determine if the individual has been the recipient of demeaning remarks or comments related to his or her protected status.

7. Review the employee's past work record and performance.

8. Obtain the employee's account of what happened, including any defenses or mitigating circumstances he or she might advance.

9. Have the appropriate decision making officer, official, or manager decide on appropriate discipline.

10. Review decision using the final filter process (see Rule 5, in this chapter).

11. Consult an employment attorney in questionable cases before final action is taken.

12. Communicate final decisions to the affected employee in a calm, confidential and thoroughly professional manner.

By following these steps, employers can assure themselves that a thorough, dispassionate, and objective investigation will be done and that disciplinary action will be taken only after a systematic analysis and a full review of all the facts and circumstances bearing on the disciplinary decision have been completed.

If this process confirms that (1) a serious violation of company rules did occur, (2) discharge is the customary penalty for such infractions, and (3) no mitigating circumstances exist to justify a lesser disciplinary action, then the discharge should be finalized and the employee told of the decision as quickly as possible. If, on the other hand, the investigation reveals that the facts were not as first suspected, that similar offenses have in the past received lesser penalties than discharge, or that there are mitigating factors, then the suspension should be lifted and the employee returned to the workforce with the appropriate disciplinary entry placed in his or her personnel file.

In some instances, further investigation may disclose that no rule infraction occurred, that the employer's initial assessment was factually incorrect, or that the conduct in question simply does not justify disciplinary action. In those cases, employees should be returned to their former position and given backpay for the period of suspension, and all disciplinary references should be removed from their personnel files.

In short, by suspending the employee rather than resorting to immediate discharge, employers gain "breathing space" to deal with what appears to be serious misconduct. Although these procedures may be time-consuming and, in some cases, costly, they are prudent measures that could save the employer thousands of dollars in backpay and damage awards, legal fees, and other related legal costs. Once again, the proverbial "ounce of prevention" will prove to be a prudent investment.

Rule 2: Get all the facts first to make sure your investigation is thorough, complete and well-documented.

Normally, the employee's supervisor, department manager, human resources director, or a member of the human resources staff investigates serious employee misconduct. Those members of management who are chosen to investigate should remember that their role is that of an investigator, not a prosecutor, and they should be open to evidence on both sides. The following list reflects the minimal steps that should be taken to ensure fair treatment during the investigation:

- Compile a thorough written report about all the facts surrounding the incident or incidents, including detailed statements from all witnesses. These should be signed and dated.
- Secure and safeguard all physical evidence.
- Review all relevant personnel and disciplinary records (both those of the employee under investigation and all similarly situated employees).
- Examine all documentation about the incident or incidents.
- Compare discipline given before for similar misconduct.
- Keep all statements, records and information confidential.
- Review the employee's entire personnel history.

Rule 3: Conduct all employee interviews with care and deliberation.

The Supreme Court in *NLRB v. Weingarten* (420 U.S. 251 (1975)) held that employees represented by a collective bargaining agent are, under certain circumstances, entitled to have a representative accompany them during any investigatory interview provided they make a timely request for such assistance. An investigatory interview has been defined as an interview the employee could reasonably believe may lead to disciplinary action. The exact circumstances triggering this right, the waiving of this right, the extent of the designated representative's right to participate, and consequences of failure to accord such a right have all been the subject of numerous decisions by the National Labor Relations Board (NLRB) as well as the courts. So, too, has the question of whether nonunion employees enjoy this same right. The board's current position on this issue is that nonunion employees are not entitled to such third-party representation. (See *E.I. Dupont De Nemours*, 128 LLRM 1233 (1988); *Sears, Roebuck & Co.*, 118 LLRM 1329 (1985).)

Giving the employee under investigation an opportunity to be heard is an important aspect of any comprehensive investigation. Frequently, the employee will present an alibi or defense that the employer had not previously considered. No matter how "off the wall" such an alibi or defense may appear to be, it is important for the investigator to seriously consider its credibility, examine its reliability and evaluate its legitimacy.

In interviewing the employee under investigation, adopt an investigative attitude and approach, not an accusatory or adversarial one. At this stage of the investigation, the interviewer should be open-minded and in search of the facts. If employees perceive that the interviewer has not prejudged the matter and is willing to listen to their side of the story, they will undoubtedly be more cooperative. On the other hand, if the employees believe that the investigator has already made up his or her mind, they will be much more defensive and much less likely to cooperate.

Once the investigator has gathered and reviewed the evidence; evaluated the sources; examined all relevant documentation, including the employee's personnel file and work history; compared how other similar offenses have been treated in the past; and listened to the employee's explanation of the matter, it is time for the investigator to summarize the findings and make a written recommendation. The written recommendation, in turn, should be carefully reviewed using the final filter process (see Rule 5 of this chapter).

In following the above procedure, the investigator should be particularly careful to examine the facts from the employee's point of view and anticipate legal defenses or other justifications that the employee might assert during the interview or in the future. It must then be determined whether such excuses or justifications constitute a defense to the alleged misconduct being investigated.

Rule 4: Investigate promptly—Don't delay.

If possible, an investigation of employee misconduct that may lead to discharge should be completed within 48 to 72 hours after the event or events giving rise to the investigation, and the employee should be told of the final decision within 24 to 48 hours thereafter. Of course, there may be situations when this timetable cannot be met, for example, if a key witness is unavailable or scientific testing must be done. However, the investigation should be done as quickly as possible. Unwarranted or unnecessary delay makes the investigation suspect and gives the impression that the employer is trying to build a case (when it doesn't have one to begin with) or that factors other than the merits of the case have influenced the outcome. Fairness to all concerned dictates that the investigation be started and completed quickly.

Rule 5: Always use the final filter approach.

Once the initial investigation is completed and termination is recommended, employers should conduct a *final filter review*. The purpose of the review is to analyze the investigator's findings and recommendations, determine if they are complete and accurate, and decide whether these findings and the recommendations that flow from them should be adopted, rejected, modified, or whether further investigation is needed before making a final decision.

The individual conducting the final filter review should not, if at all possible, have been previously involved in the investigation. Nor, if possible, should that person be involved in the direct line of supervision over the employee being investigated. In other words, this individual should be as unbiased and objective as possible and have a fresh outlook on the investigation and its outcome.

The duties of the "final filterer" include the following:

- Determining if the investigation is complete and returning the report and recommendations to the investigator if incomplete.

- Determining if any biases, intentional or unintentional, influenced the report and its recommendations.

- Examining the credibility of the witnesses and the accuracy of their statements.

- Evaluating all pertinent evidence bearing on the disposition of the case.

- Determining if the discharge is directly linked to a violation of written company rules or is otherwise sufficiently tied to violation of company policy for which termination is authorized.

- Judging the appropriateness of the punishment in light of the employee's entire work history and record.

- Ascertaining whether the employee in question falls into a protected category and, if so, determining whether his or her rights have been violated in any way.

- Determining whether the recommended discipline comports with the discipline awarded other employees who committed the same or similar infractions. (In other words, see that no disparate treatment has been accorded the individual in question.)

- Determining whether the discharge violates any legal obligation owed to the employee in question, that is, ensuring that the company's internal protections and procedures were afforded the employee, and that all company policies were complied with.

- Conferring with the person who has final discipline decision making authority and informing him or her of the "final filterer's" recommended action (if the person making the final decision is someone other than the individual who conducted the final filter review).

Role of the Employment Attorney

Whenever the proposed termination involves close factual questions, possible allegations of disparate treatment of protected employees, or involves significant legal questions, it is prudent to seek legal assistance *before* finalizing any termination decision. An employment attorney can complement the final filterer and serve as a safety check to make sure that the investigation is complete and that all relevant information needed to make a legally sound decision has been obtained.

Armed with a copy of the investigative report and the final filterer's recommendation, the employment attorney can help the employer evaluate whether the proposed discharge can be sustained if later challenged in court or elsewhere, or whether other disciplinary action might be more appropriate in light of applicable legal considerations. The employment attorney also can provide insight into other potentially troublesome considerations surrounding the proposed discipline, such as how the termination would affect employee morale or how it could serve as a basis for generating a class action lawsuit or possibly trigger union organizing activity. More important, the employment attorney can help evaluate the likelihood of subsequent legal action if the decision to terminate is carried out and can provide an assessment of the employer's chances of successfully defending itself against any such ensuing legal challenge.

This process can be eased by regular conferences between the employer and employment attorney. In this way the employment attorney can stay up to date on the employer's current employment policies and practices and the employer can get legal advice promptly. Employment attorneys, by virtue of their legal background and training and their experience with a broad range of employment legal issues, can provide employers with practical, common-sense answers to help them formulate legally defensible disciplinary decisions. Thus, when a potential discharge case arises, a short telephone conference may be all that is needed for the employment attorney to review the facts and give an informed, sound recommendation that will protect the employer's best interests.

Rule 6: Pinpoint the basis of the discharge.

Many employers fail to identify or articulate the reasons or basis for termination. This mistake could be fatal. Employers sometimes cite reasons for a discharge that they cannot prove or substantiate, while at the same time overlooking provable reasons that would amply justify termination.

Most employers do not give the employee a written copy of the reason for their discharge. Instead, they orally communicate the basis for the discharge and then record it somewhere in the employee's personnel file. This information is discoverable during an administrative investigation or lawsuit, and the employer should be prepared to defend its action on the basis stated.

A corollary to Rule 6: whenever possible, identify the specific rule or policy that the misconduct in question violates. The more specific the better. For instance, if the employee is terminated for absenteeism, spell out the specific provision of the absentee policy that was violated.

Rule 7: Whenever possible, inform the employee in person of the decision to terminate and the reasons behind it.

Once the final filterer has completed his or her assignment, with the aid of an employment attorney, if necessary, and the recommendation is to discharge the employee(s) in question, the management official authorized to carry out the decision should be informed. This decision maker might be anyone from the president of the company on down, but preferably should be a high-ranking executive in the organization. As stated earlier, this decision is so important and has such potentially serious consequences that only a high-level official should be allowed to exercise this authority.

Making the Decision

The decision-maker should review the entire record and consult with the investigator, final filterer, and, if necessary, the employment attorney. In rare cases, with the advice of an employment attorney, the decision-maker may wish to speak with the employee under investigation to verify certain aspects of the report or to seek additional information before making a final decision. However, this reviewing process should not be unduly prolonged.

Personally Communicating the Decision

When the employee is told about the decision to terminate the employment relationship, at least one other management official should be present. The reasons behind the decision should be explained as objectively and unemotionally as possible. This is not a time for personal recriminations, finger pointing, emotional outbursts or long, strident harangues. The decision should be announced at the outset of the meeting, followed by a brief explanation of the basis for the employer's decision. The employer representatives should avoid being drawn into a debate or confrontation, and under no circumstances should the meeting become a fault-finding session or heated argument.

Frequently, after the decision has been communicated, the employee will want to take issue with or challenge the employer's action. While the employee should be given an opportunity to "state his or her case" and "blow off steam," he or she should not be allowed to embark on a lengthy harangue or diatribe. If the meeting appears to be getting out of hand, the decision maker should end the meeting by simply stating, "We're sorry you feel that way, but that is our decision." There is no point in engaging in protracted discussion or debate. At this stage, the investigation has concluded. It has been fully reviewed, and the final decision made. The purpose of the termination meeting is simply to convey management's decision to the employee, not to rehash it.

The discharge meeting should conclude on a friendly note, with the management representative adding, "We're sorry your employment at the company had to end this way. We wish you well in the future," or a similar conciliatory closing remark.

At some point during the meeting, the employee should be told when to pick up a final paycheck and his or her termination rights should be explained. A number of states have laws specifying that terminated employees are entitled to payment of wages earned within a specified period following termination. Sometimes this may be as soon as the last workday, or in some cases the next regular payday. In addition, some states have laws that treat accrued fringe benefits such as vacation, sick leave and other paid time off or benefits as wages that must also be paid on termination. It is important to review those state requirements since many states impose stiff penalties for failure to comply. When employees collect their final paychecks, provide a complete written explanation of COBRA rights, severance pay, accrued vacation or sick leave or other fringe benefits to which the employee may be entitled.

Communicating the Termination in Writing

There may be occasions when it is not advisable to meet personally with the employee in question to convey the termination decision. In cases where the employee has a history of violence or psychological problems or where threats have been leveled at company officials, it may be prudent to avoid a personal confrontation. Workplace violence is escalating at an alarming rate and there is no reason to trigger a potentially explosive situation by requiring a troubled employee or one prone to violent outbursts to attend a meeting where emotions will undoubtedly run high and matters could easily get out of control. In these instances, prudence dictates avoiding a face-to-face confrontation.

In these cases, an employment attorney should be consulted to help draft a termination letter. Since this letter will undoubtedly be a critical piece of evidence in any post-termination legal challenge, it should be carefully drafted and accurately reflect the reasons for the discharge. The employee's final paycheck and a description of other benefits the employee may be legally entitled to should accompany the letter, or the employee should be informed when the final paycheck and this information will be forthcoming.

Conduct Following Termination

Communicating the termination decision should conclude the matter. Thereafter, no management official should
comment on the company's action, either with the discharged employee, other employees, the public, inquiring
prospective employers or other third parties. All inquiries
should be directed to the individual assigned to respond to
employment-related matters concerning current and former
employees, and that individual should scrupulously follow
the employer's established policy.

There is one possible exception to the general rule of
maintaining a policy of silence following discharge. If the
termination has caused unrest among the discharged
employee's fellow workers or if confusion or misinforma-
tion surrounds the discharge, the employer may wish to "set
the record straight." In those circumstances, before communicating any information about the termination and the reasons behind it, the employer should first consult with an
employment attorney to properly phrase any communication on the subject. Otherwise, the employer may be provid-
ing the former employee with added ammunition for
launching a legal attack.

To summarize, once the decision to terminate has been
reached, communicate it in person quickly, tactfully and
dispassionately. Then, pay the employee what he or she is
legally owed, conclude on a cordial note and discuss the
matter no further, unless absolutely essential to alleviate
employee concerns—and then only after your communication has been cleared by an employment attorney.

Rule 8: Always employ progressive discipline, keeping appropriate documentation.

Workplace disciplinary systems are grounded on the theory
of rehabilitation, not punishment. By using appropriate disciplinary measures, employers try to send a message to
errant employees and let them know their performance
must improve or more serious consequences will follow.
The employer's disciplinary measures should be constructive and they should be directed at letting employees know
that their conduct or performance has slipped below acceptable norms and that improvement is both necessary and

expected. If the employee heeds the constructive counseling, well and good. The caution signal will have accomplished its purpose, and a potential employment problem will have been averted. If the employer's counseling efforts go unheeded, stronger measures may have to be used to impress on the employee the seriousness of the situation and the need for immediate corrective action.

In a unionized setting, arbitrators are frequently called on to determine whether the grievant has been terminated for *just cause*. In fact, there are thousands of arbitration decisions defining what constitutes just cause, given the facts of the individual case. In determining the question of just cause, arbitrators frequently examine whether the principles of progressive discipline have been followed. These principles require employers to gradually increase the level of the discipline administered, until the employee is sufficiently put on notice that future transgressions will result in termination. Thus, employees are made aware that their conduct or performance is considered unacceptable and that they must improve or face the prospect of termination. If employees continue to ignore these warning signals, arbitrators generally uphold their discharge.

Although nonunion employers are not under any legal obligation to follow a just cause standard (unless they have imposed this standard on themselves by their written policies), they should, nonetheless, follow these same principles. As is frequently the case, this is an instance in which legally acceptable practices and sound management procedures coincide. Encouraging employees to improve their performance through progressive discipline simply makes good business sense, particularly in light of the investment that the employer has already made in recruiting, hiring and training the employee, to say nothing of the costs that would be incurred to hire a replacement.

Both government investigators and reviewing courts tend to uphold an employer's disciplinary action if it establishes a systematic foundation of counseling and warnings which clearly state that future misconduct would jeopardize the employee's continued employment. Such a warning notice is often given in a "last chance" letter, stating that the employee is being given one final opportunity to conform his or her conduct to acceptable norms of behavior or performance, or face termination.

A last chance letter should contain a brief summary of the employee's disciplinary and performance history, recount previous attempts to inform the employee of the seriousness of the situation, and emphasize clearly the need for immediate reform. It should end by plainly spelling out that further misconduct or continued unacceptable performance will result in termination. Because a last chance letter is an important document that could play a key role in any subsequent legal contest, it should be reviewed by an employment attorney before it is given to the employee.

A last chance letter should be personally delivered to the employee during a meeting called for this purpose, and another management official should witness its transmission. At this meeting, the seriousness of the situation should be forcefully reiterated and the employee should be asked to acknowledge that he or she understands that any further impermissible conduct or unsatisfactory performance will result in termination. This last chance meeting also gives an employer the opportunity to observe the employee's reaction to the ultimatum, and may indicate whether the employee will challenge subsequent disciplinary action. If a challenge appears likely, then an employment attorney should be consulted before any subsequent disciplinary decision is finalized. (See Rule 5 of this chapter.)

Rule 9: When you are done with your homework—go for it.

Throughout this book, the great financial costs and other serious consequences associated with improper and illegal employment termination decisions have been stressed. However, this discussion would not be complete without observing that sometimes an even more costly termination decision can be the one that is never made.

As expensive as an ill-advised termination decision could be, the decision to terminate an unsatisfactory employee may prove far less costly than continuing to employ someone whose performance is not only unacceptable, but whose continued presence in the workforce undermines employee morale and creates a bad example for others to follow. Some employees not only fail to abide by established rules of conduct or conform to established performance standards, but they also constantly "bad mouth" the employer and its policies to anyone who will listen and are not averse to letting it be known that the employer is giving them and the rest of the employees "a raw deal." These individuals can cause incalculable damage to an organization and must be separated for everyone's benefit. For some inexplicable reason, many employers delay confronting employees like this until it is too late. For instance, despite the fact that an employee like the one described may have a work history that would provide ample basis for disciplinary termination, many employers procrastinate. Instead of documenting the employee's failings and following progressive disciplinary principles, they drift along, reluctant to "bite the bullet."

Later, after this chronically malcontent employee foments a union organizing campaign, instigates a vexatious OSHA complaint, files a spurious workers' compensation claim or triggers other unwarranted charges with a government agency, the employer finally takes decisive action, only to find that it waited too long. When such a termination is later challenged, as it inevitably will be, the investigating agency will undoubtedly conclude that the real reason behind the discharge is employer retaliation because the employee exercised his or her legally protected rights. (See Chapter II.) The investigator's conclusion will be bolstered by the fact that the employee's conduct before the discharge was no worse than it had been throughout his or her employment history. Since the employer had not acted to terminate the employee earlier, the investigator will undoubtedly conclude that the real cause of the termination could only be the employee's having engaged in legally protected activity and that any other reason cited by the employer is nothing more than a pretext. Consequently, once employees have engaged in some legally protected activity or exercised a legally protected right, their termination will be considerably complicated, regardless of how bad their previous work record may have been or how justifiable termination might otherwise be.

Failing to separate this type of employee from the workforce at an appropriate time costs the employer considerable money in lost productivity, through both the employee's substandard performance and the poor example he or she undoubtedly sets for other employees. Of course, such individuals may challenge any decision involving their termination regardless of when the decision is made. Yet, even though the termination decision may be very costly, in many instances failure to take timely and appropriate decisive action will be far more costly in the long run.

Rule 10: Beware of the setup.

By this time, the reader is undoubtedly aware that after the termination conference, the next meeting with the ex-employee may well take place in an attorney's office. What most employers do not realize, however, is that in many cases employees have seen the handwriting on the wall and retained an attorney before their actual termination. Consequently, employers should become aware of telltale signs that indicate they are being set up. Requests by employees to see or copy their personnel records and possibly those of other employees, requests that the employer put statements in writing, conversations focusing on the employee's protected status, detailed inquiries about disciplinary procedures or company policies and benefits, questions concerning comparative treatment with regard to other employees and other similar actions may be indications that employees have been furnished with a detailed game plan to put the employer on the defensive. Employers are well advised to consult their own legal counsel once they determine this to be the case.

In setup situations, employers must follow exactly the same procedures with the problem employee as they do with everyone else. One of the worst things that an employer can do under these circumstances is to single out the employee in question for special attention or treatment. Such conduct will merely reinforce the employee's contention that he or she is being subjected to a double standard. If it can be established that the employee has been singled out for special treatment, the employer's motives will be impugned and subsequent disciplinary action will be challenged on the basis that the "employer was out to get me." Plaintiff's attorneys like nothing better than to portray their client as the victim of an employer inquisition or vendetta.

There is no reason to panic if it is discovered that an employee is laying a foundation to contest future disciplinary action. By following the procedures outlined earlier in this chapter, employers can achieve the same amount of success in defending against legal challenges by counseled employees as noncounseled ones. The key is to not overreact by making the employee a designated target. Instead, the employer should continue to apply to the employee in question the same rules and procedures that are applied to all other employees.

CHAPTER V

COLEMAN'S CARDINAL RULES FOR TERMINATIONS FOR EMPLOYMENT PROBLEMS

Misconduct is not the only reason an employee may be slated for termination. Sometimes an employee has not broken any rules or violated any policies, but is unable or unwilling to perform the job as the employer expects. Many of Coleman's Cardinal Rules from Chapter IV apply here, and here are some more basic rules that any employer should follow before making a final decision to terminate an employee for poor performance:

Rule 1: Never summarily discharge.

As in situations involving employee misconduct, it is essential that an employer contemplating the termination of an employee for performance-related reasons carefully consider the decision. Even when an employee's neglect of his or her duties or on-the-job mistakes have severe consequences, termination on-the-spot is not advisable. If necessary, the employee can be "suspended subject to discharge pending further investigation." But whether or not the employee is suspended, an employer considering terminating an employee based on performance should do the following:

1. Complete a thorough factual investigation.

2. Obtain written statements from the employee's supervisors and/or other witnesses, and from the employee. The employee's statement should include any explanations he or she has for the alleged performance problems.

3. If the employee is in a protected category, determine whether he or she has been the victim of disparate treatment. Determine if the individual has been the recipient of demeaning remarks or comments related to his or her protected status.

4. Review the employee's past work record and performance.

5. Have the appropriate decision-making officer, official or manager decide on appropriate discipline.

6. Review the decision using the final filter process (see Chapter IV, Rule 5).

7. Consult an employment attorney in questionable cases before final action is taken.

8. Communicate the final decision to the affected employee in a calm, confidential and thoroughly professional manner.

By following these simple steps, an employer can minimize its exposure to a lawsuit by an employee terminated for alleged performance problems. Although this process requires a good deal of work and can be expensive, it will go a long way toward avoiding unnecessary, costly and time-consuming litigation.

Rule 2: Get all the facts first to make sure your investigation is thorough, complete and well-documented.

An employee cannot be expected to perform in accordance with standards that have never been communicated to him or her. Thus, it is critical to ascertain whether the employee has been given some objective performance standards which are not being met. In this connection, it is important to review the written description of the employee's duties to determine whether it accurately reflects the employee's actual duties. Too often, job duties evolve over time, until they bear little or no resemblance to the written job description that is in place for the position. If this is so, the employer will have a much more difficult time proving that any termination was justified by the employee's performance problems. Similarly, the employer will have problems of proof if no job description exists for the position.

Where a job description does exist, the employer also must be able to demonstrate that it was actually shared with the employee. Ideally, the employer will have a signed acknowledgment form from the employee which states that the employee received the job description. If this is not possible, then a management employee should be in a position to testify that he or she presented the description to the employee and/or discussed its contents with him or her. When no job description exists, the employer must be prepared to show that management communicated specific responsibilities, tasks or goals to the employee, which were not carried out or met.

These rules, with Rules 9 and 10, were thoroughly discussed in Chapter IV.

Rule 3: Conduct all employee interviews with care and deliberation.

Rule 4: Investigate promptly—don't delay.

Rule 5: Always use the final filter approach.

Rule 6: Pinpoint the basis of the discharge.

Rule 7: Whenever possible, inform the employee in person of the decision to terminate and the reasons behind it.

Rule 8: Always follow progressive discipline, keeping appropriate documentation.

Many employers have adopted policies that provide for the "progressive discipline" of employees whose performance is below acceptable standards. The policies typically provide that the employee identified as a problem performer will be subject to verbal and written warnings and paid and unpaid suspensions before the more severe measure of termination is taken. Where they exist, such policies must be carefully followed. If they are not, then discharged employees are in a position to argue that the employer breached a contractual obligation to undertake progressive discipline before terminating them. Moreover, if such policies are not uniformly applied (*i.e.*, similar penalties are not meted out for similar infractions), then protected category employees who are treated less favorably than non-protected category employees will have ammunition for a discrimination lawsuit.

But even if there is no system of progressive discipline in place, it is good policy and good business to terminate based on performance only after progressive discipline has failed. In a legal context, the issue is one of fairness. Most courts will be more inclined to uphold a discharge if an employee has been given warnings and a chance to improve before being terminated. And the fact that any termination constitutes a loss of the substantial investment made in each employee hired and trained also favors a policy designed to salvage errant employees.

Finally, in a unionized setting, an employer must have "just cause" to terminate an employee for performance reasons. In deciding whether there is "just cause," arbitrators routinely analyze whether progressive discipline has been implemented. If it has not, then the arbitrator is likely to determine that the employee was not "on notice" that his or her conduct could result in termination and that reinstatement (with full backpay) is warranted.

Rule 9: When you are done with your homework—go for it.

Rule 10: Beware of the setup.

For a thorough discussion of Rules 9 and 10, see Chapter IV.

CHAPTER VI

COLEMAN'S CARDINAL RULES FOR CONDUCTING A LAYOFF/REDUCTION IN FORCE (RIF)

An employee's misconduct or performance problems are not the only reasons that an employer may elect to terminate the worker. Often employers have to make difficult termination decisions when the company is forced to cut back on its workforce for business-related reasons. Although many of the same steps should be taken in layoff situations as are taken when terminating an employee for misconduct or poor performance, several additional considerations apply to layoffs as well. An employer planning and implementing a layoff should keep the following considerations in mind:

Rule 1: Monitor the effect of the layoff on protected category employees.

Employees who are selected for layoff often believe they were wrongly selected, and that the company had some ulterior motive for terminating them. To the extent that the employee is a member of a protected category under federal, state and/or local anti-discrimination laws, the employee may suspect that his or her status played a part in the termination. These suspicions, even if entirely unfounded, may result in the filing of a charge of discrimination with the appropriate administrative agency, or the institution of a lawsuit. The employer then will be called upon to defend its layoff decisions before the agency or court by demonstrating that the decisions were based on sound business considerations.

To prepare for such an eventuality, an employer involved in the planning of a layoff should be careful to analyze the impact of the selection process on protected category employees. Is the layoff, as planned, likely to result in the termination of a disproportionate number of women, minorities or workers age 40 and older? If so, the employer would be well-advised to ensure that the termination decisions can be defended on grounds of legitimate business considerations, and are not intended to have a discriminatory effect. While layoffs can still be accomplished, even if they create an adverse impact on protected category employees, the employer is well-advised to document the decision-making process so that, if later called upon to do so, it will be in a position to draw a direct link between the business objectives that the layoff was designed to achieve and the decision to lay off specific workers. The advice of an employment attorney can be invaluable in helping to ensure not only that the decision-making process is free from improper considerations, but (equally important) that the employer will be in a position to *prove* that fact should it later be required to do so.

Often, an entire department or several departments are eliminated when operations are changed, or when business or financial reasons dictate. Any disparate impact such decisions may have is normally easier to defend than in the more common situation, *i.e.*, when only some employees in a given department are discharged. In such cases, the danger that an employer will be held responsible for discriminatory layoffs is magnified because the discharged employee can point to another employee and say, "Why not him or her instead?" An employer's potential exposure is also magnified when individual managers are permitted to make recommendations regarding the laying off of individuals in their departments. In such cases, it is always possible that the prejudices of the manager (for which the employer ultimately could be held legally responsible) will play a role in the layoff choices. In all situations involving partial layoffs of a department and in all situations in which managers select (or have significant input into selecting) who will be laid off, the work history of any employee selected for layoff should be reviewed carefully to ensure that no improper considerations influenced the decision to terminate the employee.

Rule 2: Determine whether the layoff is subject to federal, state and/or local laws requiring notice to the employees and others that the layoff will occur.

Congress, many state legislatures and local governments have passed numerous laws which place some limits on an employer's right to close or relocate plants, or to lay off large groups of employees. These laws typically require the employer planning sizable layoffs to provide advance notice to the employees affected, the union representing them (if any), and specified government agencies/officials.

On the federal level, employers must consider the effect of the Worker Adjustment and Retraining Notification Act (WARN). WARN does not apply to all employers. It applies *only* to employers who employ 100 or more full-time workers or 100 or more full- and part-time employees, who work at least 4,000 hours per week in aggregate straight time. Moreover, employers covered by WARN are required to give advance notice of a plant closing or mass layoff *only* if 50 or more workers will be affected. But even employers who are not required to give notice of layoffs under WARN should always check state and local laws to determine if they are required to give notice under those laws. Moreover, employers subject to WARN should review state and local laws to ensure that they do not impose stricter or additional requirements.

WARN requires covered employers to give advance notice of permanent layoffs, mass closings or employment loss if either 500 full-time employees or 50 or more full-time employees constituting at least 33 percent of the workforce are affected. To trigger advance notice, a layoff must affect at least 50 workers and 33 percent of the workforce. The layoff must be permanent or exceed six months. Advance notice is also required if employees have their hours of work cut by more than 50 percent during each month of any six-month period.

Employers covered by WARN must give 60 days' advance notice to each employee affected by a plant closing or layoff. The notice should be mailed to the employee's home or inserted in paycheck envelopes. Verbal notice, general notices or bulletin board notices are not sufficient. Written notice also must be given to representatives of the employees' union (if any), the state Dislocated Worker Unit and the chief elected official of the employer's local government.

Generally, the notice should contain the name and address of the facility, the names and addresses of the affected employees, the employees' job titles and social security numbers, the name of the union and the chief elected official of any union representing the affected employees, clear identification of the expected date when the plant closing or mass layoff will commence, and whether the closing or layoff is temporary. The notice also should advise of the existence of any applicable bumping rights, and should identify a company official to contact for further information.

Employers who fail to give the proper notice under WARN may be required to pay (1) backpay and benefits to each aggrieved employee for each day of the violation, up to a maximum of 60 days; (2) attorneys' fees if the aggrieved employee is the prevailing party; and (3) a maximum fine of $500 per day for each day of the violation up to a maximum of 60 days (or $30,000), unless payment is made to each aggrieved employee within 21 days of the shutdown or layoff. WARN does not provide for injunctive relief, so an employer cannot be compelled to keep a plant open or to retain employees.

WARN provides three exceptions to the notice requirement. The notice requirements may be reduced in a plant closing situation if such notice would have precluded the employer from obtaining capital or new business that would have enabled the employer to avoid or to postpone the closing. This exception does not apply to mass layoff situations.

Advance notice also is not required if the closing or layoff was not reasonably foreseeable at the time notice was required. These circumstances must be sudden, dramatic and unexpected. For example, a sudden strike at a major supplier, economic downturn or the loss of a major customer may be construed as unforeseeable circumstances. If the closing or layoff is caused by natural disasters such as flood, earthquakes or drought, advance notice also is not required.

Finally, WARN does not apply when employers hire employees with the express understanding that the project is temporary or of limited duration. Thus, short-term or specific-duration contracts do not trigger WARN notice

requirements. Also excluded from coverage are plant reloca-
tions or consolidation of businesses if, prior to the consolidation or relocation, the employer offers a transfer to the
affected employees.

As should be apparent from the above description, the
requirements of WARN and the potential requirements of
state and local laws make it essential that employers contemplating a mass layoff or plant closing consult an employment attorney. Making a determination regarding whether
WARN and/or other laws apply to a given situation and, if
so, the requirements of compliance, can be tricky, and the
consequences of "getting it wrong" can be severe.

Rule 3: Review and follow all contractual obligations relating to layoffs.

An employer implementing layoffs may have certain contractual obligations in the event of a layoff. For example,
some employers have written policies which provide that, in
the event of a layoff, terminations will be based on seniority.
Similarly, many employers also have policies which provide
for the payment of severance pay to laid-off employees.
Other applicable policies also may exist. If an employer fails
to abide by any of these policies, an employee may sue the
employer for breach of contract. Failure to abide by the
terms of a severance pay plan also may constitute a violation of the Employee Retirement Income Security Act
(ERISA) because severance pay plans are employee welfare
benefit plans under ERISA. In addition, if an employer
implements layoff-related policies in a way that has the purpose or effect of discriminating against "protected category"
employees, a discrimination charge or lawsuit may ensue. It
therefore is critically important for employers implementing
layoffs to follow all policies relating to layoffs and to apply
them in a non-discriminatory manner.

If the employees are unionized, the employer must
ascertain whether the union contract contains provisions relevant to layoffs. Union contracts often provide for layoffs
based on seniority, and these provisions must be honored or
the employer may be subject to a claim that its layoffs resulted in an unfair labor practice. An employer has a duty to
bargain concerning the effects that a decision to go out of

business will have on bargaining unit employees, and in some cases may have a duty to bargain about the decision itself.

Rule 4: Take steps to minimize the potential negative effects of a layoff.

A layoff is a traumatic event, both for the employees who are terminated and for those employees who remain. Employees who are laid off will not soon forget the manner in which they were treated "on the way out." The reputation of the employer in the community will be injured or enhanced depending on what those who are laid off tell others about the manner in which they were terminated. By treating employees fairly and courteously in a layoff situation, an employer also can minimize its exposure to legal challenges. Employees who are given information and assistance to help them get back on their feet when they are terminated will have less need to sue the employer and will be less inclined to do so. Finally, because a layoff also reminds employees who are not affected by the layoff that their employment is not guaranteed, the layoff can cause a great deal of stress among the remaining workforce. A real sense of "that could have been me" is not uncommon in layoff situations. The treatment of employees who are laid off will be closely watched by remaining employees. To minimize damage to employee morale, it is essential that the employer carefully implement the layoff.

Laid-off employees are entitled to receive unemployment compensation as long as they are not reemployed. If a large number of employees have been laid off, and/or they are unemployed for a long period of time, the effect on an employer's legally required contributions to the unemployment fund can be substantial. The sooner employees are reemployed after a layoff, the sooner they will be removed from the unemployment rolls. In addition, employees who are rapidly reemployed are less inclined to sue their former employer. It may make sense for an employer to provide some form of outplacement service to laid-off employees to help expedite their search for alternative employment. At a minimum, the employer should offer employees information about state or local agencies that may offer placement assistance.

Although unemployment insurance is available to laid-off employees, such benefits are less than the employees earned while at work. To make the transition a smoother one, an employer who does not already have an applicable severance pay plan might consider granting severance pay to terminated employees. Doing so may create obligations under ERISA, however, and the potential for discriminatory results of an *ad hoc* severance plan abound. It is advisable for the employer to contact an employment attorney to evaluate the employer's proposed severance pay plan in any layoff situation.

Rule 5: Make certain that any termination agreements are fair, voluntary and based on full notice and disclosure.

Employers are frequently willing to pay departing employees severance pay or other compensation to which they are not otherwise legally entitled in exchange for a release or waiver of any claims that the employees may have (or think they have) against the employer. The employer must be aware, however, that such releases or waivers may not be upheld by a court if it appears that they were not voluntarily made, that the employee did not understand what he or she was giving up by signing the document or if the employee did not receive anything in exchange for signing the release or waiver. To help ensure that a waiver or release will be upheld, an employer should:

1. Give the employee something of value to which he or she would not otherwise have been entitled (such as severance pay or outplacement assistance) in exchange for signing the release or waiver.

2. Allow the employee a reasonable period of time to consider the waiver or release before obtaining his or her signature.

3. Permit the employee to consult with his or her own legal counsel before executing the release.

4. Draft the agreement in plain English rather than "legalese" so that it can be understood by the employee, and explain the significance of the waiver or release to the employee in the presence of another management witness. Answer any of the employee's questions

to make certain that he or she understands the agreement and its effect.

One additional word of caution is warranted when workers age 40 and older are involved. The federal Older Workers Benefit Protection Act (OWBPA) contains some very strict guidelines relating to the effectiveness of waivers relating to age discrimination claims. Under OWBPA, employees must be given the opportunity to consult with a lawyer, must be given 21 days to consider the waiver and must have 7 days to revoke the waiver after signing it if they change their minds. An employer must exercise extreme care when negotiating releases from workers age 40 and older. The pitfalls of failing to provide proper safeguards can be devastating: some courts have held that an employee who signs an ineffective waiver can keep the severance pay given in exchange for the waiver and *still sue* the employer for age discrimination. It is critical that the employer have any release prepared and/or reviewed by an employment attorney.

Rule 6: Implement the decision.

Once an employee has been selected for termination in a layoff, the decision should be communicated to him or her personally. The steps which should be followed are generally the same as those set forth in Rule 7 of Chapter IV. The objects of the meeting at which the employee is advised of his termination are (1) to communicate the basis of the decision to the employee and (2) to communicate the details of the termination to the employee (*i.e.*, when employment will cease, when a final paycheck will issue, entitlement to accrued benefits such as vacation or sick leave, availability of severance pay, COBRA benefits, availability of outplacement services and existence of state/local agencies that might assist in helping the employee to find another job). Because of the amount of information which is being shared with the employee, and because it is essential that there be no dispute as to exactly what was communicated, the employer should present the employee with a letter that sets forth all of these details. Finally, the employer should have a management witness present, and the meeting should not devolve into a "debate" regarding why an employee was "wrongly selected" for layoff. The meeting should end on a positive note, with the employer advising the employee: "We regret this measure became necessary, and we wish you well in the future." If, for any reason, the employer believes that an employee may be prone to violence, a face-to-face meeting may be inadvisable. In that instance, a properly drafted letter will suffice.

Chapter VII

Post-Termination Considerations

Typically, in the aftermath of an employee layoff or termination, employers must address several related issues: payment of wages, COBRA benefits, unemployment benefits, reference checks and limits on liability. A discussion of each issue follows.

Payment of Wages

When employees are laid off or terminated, the employer must ensure that they are paid all compensation due them in accordance with the applicable state law. State wage payment laws typically require that a final paycheck be given to a terminated employee by a specific time. Depending on the state, that time may be the last day of work, the next regular billing cycle, or within a specific number of days after termination. The employer must also determine whether accrued vacation or sick leave constitutes "wages" that must be paid to a departing employee under state law. When an employer fails to pay terminated employees all that they are owed promptly, state wage board inquiries and/or investigations, as well as substantial penalties, may result.

COBRA Benefits

In any termination or layoff, the question of whether to extend federal COBRA benefits to employees arises. The federal COBRA statute requires employers with health insurance plans that cover 20 or more employees to offer continued health insurance coverage to terminated employees and their qualified beneficiaries. The purpose of COBRA is to provide a health insurance coverage "bridge" for terminated employees and their dependents by ensuring the continued availability of post-termination health insurance at an affordable group rate for a finite period. Specifically, as long as the employee pays all associated premiums on time, the law permits the employee and his or her beneficiaries to continue to receive health coverage at a group rate for 18 months after termination.

Several points about COBRA warrant particular mention. First, the employer must be certain to send the required COBRA notice within the prescribed period to the terminated employee and his or her qualified beneficiaries. Failure to provide an adequate notice on time may result in legal liability, including substantial penalties and adverse tax consequences. Second, in situations involving the discharge of an employee "for cause," employers should resist the temptation to punish the employee by denying COBRA coverage. Although the law permits an employer to deny COBRA benefits to an employee who has engaged in *gross misconduct*, that term is not defined in the statute and the courts have interpreted it extremely narrowly. In general, gross misconduct will not be found unless an employee was actually attempting to damage the employer—for instance, if the employee was embezzling funds. The employee's violation of the employer's work rules and policies—even if the violations were blatant and established just cause for the termination—typically will not constitute gross misconduct and therefore will not justify denial of COBRA benefits. As a rule of thumb, it is wise to extend COBRA benefits to all terminated employees to avoid potentially costly litigation over whether the employee was terminated for gross misconduct.

Finally, the employer must be careful not to prematurely cut off an employee's COBRA benefits because of a late premium payment. The law provides a 30-day grace period for late payments and as a matter of practice a warning notice should be sent to an employee before benefits are severed. A warning notice will prevent employees from later alleging that the delinquency was somehow justified and that their benefits should be restored and/or that the employer should be held liable for health-related bills they incurred during a lapse in coverage.

Unemployment Benefits

The first instinct of many employees who are laid off or discharged is to apply for unemployment compensation. Many

claims for unemployment compensation are clearly merito-
rious and no challenge is appropriate. Less frequently, however, employees who quit or are discharged for cause will
file unemployment claims. In such cases, the employer must
decide whether to contest the claim.

The decision to challenge an unemployment insurance
claim can be a costly one. Unemployment compensation is
the last immediately available source of income for many
former employees. If employees already feel they were
unjustly terminated, they may be driven over the edge by
the employer's decision to challenge their right to receive
these benefits. Backed against the wall, employees who
might not otherwise have sued the employer over their discharge may decide to do so.

In addition to that risk, challenging an unemployment
claim results in lost staff time. Employees who have first-
hand knowledge of the circumstances surrounding a termination will be required to appear as witnesses at any
unemployment compensation hearing. Whatever time the
employees spend at a hearing will be lost time at work.
And, if legal counsel is obtained, those legal fees must be
factored in as well.

Invariably, employees will appeal a denial of unemployment benefits because it costs them nothing to do so. The
employer, on the other hand, must ask itself whether it
wants to retain counsel and/or expend the time of its own
staff in defending against an appeal.

Another problem also may arise. The witnesses whom
the employer will present in an employment compensation
hearing are themselves employees. They may be hesitant to
testify against former employees and may refuse to do so.
Sometimes the employees will testify—but in favor of the
former employee. If either of these situations occurs, the
employer may unwittingly create yet another problem if the
employee-witness is later terminated or if negative employment actions are taken against that witness. Unemployment
compensation statutes typically contain provisions that pro-
hibit employers from retaliating against employees for their
participation in an unemployment compensation hearing.
The witness may claim—in a lawsuit—that he or she was
retaliated against either for refusing to testify and/or for tes-
tifying against the employer.

Of course, employers faced with a questionable unemployment compensation claim may justifiably decide to contest the application. In particular, in industries characterized by high employee turnover, it may be good business in the long term to contest such claims. The volume of claims filed in high-turnover businesses can cause the amount of money that the employer is required to pay into the unemployment insurance fund to rise precipitously. In the long run, it may behoove the employer to make it known in the community—by regularly challenging claims of questionable validity—that it is not a soft touch for unemployment claims.

The decision to contest or not contest unemployment claims should not be made for the wrong reasons, however. Many employers operate under the misconception that they must meet the allegations made by an employee submitting an unemployment compensation claim or be bound by them in later litigation. If an employee states that he or she was terminated because of employment discrimination, for example, many employers believe that a failure to deny those allegations will prejudice them in a later lawsuit over the employee's termination. However, often unemployment compensation laws expressly provide that findings made in the context of a claim for unemployment compensation are inadmissible in a subsequent employment-related lawsuit. Employers should check the unemployment laws in their own states to determine the extent to which failing to respond to an employee's allegations in an unemployment compensation claim might be used in subsequent litigation. In states where the facts and issues that arise in unemployment proceedings *will* have a conclusive effect in later litigation, employers should proceed with special caution—and with the advice of an employment attorney.

Reference Checking

An employer who receives a reference request from a former employee's potential employer must proceed with care. Failure to exercise such care could land the employer on the wrong side of a lawsuit for defamation, interference with prospective contractual relations, discrimination, retaliation and any number of other claims. Obviously, if the employee was involuntarily terminated, the potential for a lawsuit is greatly enhanced. An involuntarily terminated employee may feel that the employer or one or more of its employees is "out to get him"—first by terminating him or her and then by "blackballing" him or her through the reference-checking process. Whether based on fact or not, such a perception can be all the employee needs to obtain a lawyer and file suit.

There are two basic policies that employers can use in dealing with reference checking. The easiest and most reliable method for avoiding liability is to limit responses to reference checks. Most commonly, employers will reveal only the employee's dates of employment, positions held and salary. In addition, to avoid the problem that may arise if an unauthorized employee gives a reference that may then be attributed to the organization, it is imperative that the policy clearly define *who* in the organization is authorized to respond to reference checks. Depending on the size of the organization, it may be the office manager or the HR department. Nobody other than the designated individual(s) should provide information regarding former employees. It also is good policy not to respond to telephone inquiries, but to require written inquiries instead. In that way, employers can avoid former employees' later claims that information was given *not* to potential employers, but to bill collectors or other third parties not entitled to private information about their employment. Finally, once a reference checking policy is adopted, it must be communicated to all employees to make sure that no unauthorized references are given out, and it must be uniformly applied. Unless these last steps are taken, the effectiveness of the policy will be undermined.

The second basic approach employers can take is to agree to provide more expansive references, but *only* if the employee signs a properly worded release that has been reviewed and approved by an employment attorney. These releases, however, are not sufficient protection standing alone. For one thing, it is doubtful that they would be effective if employees alleged an employer had maliciously "blackballed" them by saying untrue things in a reference. Therefore, when adopting this policy, employers must still control what is said in replying to a reference check and they must limit the people entitled to give references. This practice is needed to avoid having someone "say the wrong thing." To exert still further control, the employer also might choose to give written references only. This practice would' avoid disputes over what exactly was said about the former employee. Whatever policy is adopted, however, it still is imperative that it be communicated to all employees and that it be uniformly applied.

Limits on Liability

An employer who takes all the above precautions and is still sued for discriminatory discharge has a new weapon in its arsenal in the wake of the U.S. Supreme Court's recent decision in *McKennon v. Nashville Banner Publishing Co.* That case establishes that if a former employee files a discrimination suit against an employer, the employer may minimize its potential liability through use of the *after-acquired evidence* defense. Before the *Nashville Banner* case, it was unclear whether evidence brought to light by an employer while defending itself against a claim of discriminatory discharge—evidence that would have provided a valid basis for terminating the employee had it been known to the employer—could constitute a complete defense to a former employee's discrimination lawsuit.

Plaintiffs' lawyers had argued that courts should not permit such discoveries to exonerate an employer who had discriminatorily discharged an employee. Defense lawyers, on the other hand, had contended that the fact the employee could have been discharged for cause before the discriminatory discharge occurred should immunize an employer from suit. The Supreme Court in *Nashville Banner* mapped out a middle ground between those two approaches.

The Court ruled that an employee alleging discriminatory discharge under the Age Discrimination in Employment Act (ADEA) is *not* barred from all relief even if the employer later discovers evidence that would have justified the employee's termination had the employer known of it at the time. But the Supreme Court ruled that such after-acquired evidence of the employee's wrongdoing *should* have an impact on the employee's remedy. Specifically, the Court ruled that the employee's relief generally would be restricted to backpay, calculated from the date of the discriminatory discharge to the date the after-acquired evidence was discovered. The Court also ruled that reinstatement would be an inappropriate remedy for such employees. Allowing a little "wiggle room," the Court also noted that these rules might be altered somewhat in "extraordinary circumstances."

In the aftermath of *Nashville Banner*, several points have become clear. First and most important, it is apparent that it is the employer's burden to establish that the misconduct it has raised as a defense, if previously known, would have resulted in the employee's termination. Frequently, such misconduct will be related to misrepresentations made by employees on their employment applications regarding their qualifications. Therefore, employers must be careful to establish clearly articulated policies regarding the falsification of application information and to spell out what other types of misconduct will result in termination. Employers also must be prepared to demonstrate that they have consistently enforced these policies. Otherwise, the courts are likely to view an employer's later reliance on the after-acquired evidence defense with a jaundiced eye, and the employer will be open to the full range of damages available under the discrimination laws.

CHAPTER VIII

A FINAL WORD

The decision to terminate an employee is one of the most potentially costly decisions an employer can make. The backpay meter begins to run the moment an employee is terminated and continues until any and all legal proceedings are resolved. Because the administrative and judicial processes are time consuming, this could take months, or even years. In addition to traditional backpay and reinstatement, employers who wrongfully terminate an employee may be subject to punitive or exemplary damages designed to punish or make an example of the employer for its illegal conduct. Frequently, such punitive damages awards alone total millions of dollars. Finally, an employer forced to defend itself against such attacks will spend considerable sums of money on attorney's fees and related legal costs, as well as valuable time and resources in preparing its defense. Indeed, because of the costs associated with defending against employment-related claims by former employees, it is often said that an employer who is sued loses, whatever the final judicial outcome. Therefore, employers should take appropriate steps to decrease their exposure to legal attacks by former employees and to reduce the severity of these legal challenges if they occur.

Over the past 20 years, the employment relationship has become increasingly regulated by legislation on the federal, state and local levels, circumscribing management's once-sacrosanct freedom to fire. In addition, the courts are steadily eroding the traditional right of employers to discharge employees previously considered to be employed at will. This continuing erosion of the employment-at-will doctrine is being accelerated by judicial acceptance of a number of new legal theories, all of which impose limitations on management's right to terminate the employment relationship. These judicially crafted theories include setting aside employee terminations on the grounds that employee handbooks created implied contractual obligations or on the grounds that public policy considerations precluded termination.

Employers are rightly concerned about the growing maze of laws restricting their freedom to make important employment decisions, particularly the decision to discharge employees. But prudent employers can still retain control of their employment decisions and successfully repel challenges to them by doing their homework before, rather than after, the termination decision is made and implemented. By exercising sound judgment, analyzing comparative disciplinary actions in the workplace, and conducting a thorough, fact-intensive investigation before making a discharge decision, employers can make termination decisions that are fully justified and able to withstand legal challenge.

To order additional copies
of this book, call the
SHRM Order Desk
at (800) 444-5006.